T0197644

319%

RICHARD ZUREKK

Copyright © 2018 by Richard Zurekk. 780561

All rights reserved. No part of this book may be reproduced
or transmitted in any form or by any means, electronic or
mechanical, including photocopying, recording, or by any
information storage and retrieval system, without permission
in writing from the copyright owner.

To order additional copies of this book, contact:
Xlibris
844-714-8691
www.Xlibris.com
Orders@Xlibris.com

ISBN: Softcover   978-1-9845-3355-5
         Hardcover   978-1-9845-3356-2
         EBook   978-1-9845-3354-8

Print information available on the last page

Rev. date: 08/29/2020

CONTENTS

Preface v

Introduction. vii

Chapter 1   Rules to trade by in Equity markets as well as the Commodity markets. 1

Chapter 2   Researching. 4

Chapter 3   Risk and Perspective 17

Chapter 4   Buying 20

Chapter 5   Selling. 23

Chapter 6   Introduction to the Next Level 25

Chapter 7   Commodities Summary 26

Chapter 8   Corn (Symbol ZC) 28

Chapter 9   Wheat (Symbol ZW) 31

Chapter 10   Research on Automated Trading (Commodities and Stocks). 34

Chapter 11   Overall Summary 35

Appendix A 39

Appendix B 41

PREFACE

You will want to buy this book if:

1. You would like to check to see that your adviser[1] mostly has your best interests in mind
2. Learn some basic techniques for measuring risk
3. Learn some techniques for identifying fake news
4. Learn some basic techniques for buying and selling stock
5. Learn some basic strategies for trading commodities
6. Get some basic macro-economic outlooks
7. Obtain the ability to ask me questions, including complex commodity strategies
8. Looking to bring down your costs and increase your returns
9. Raise or decrease the amount of risk you are exposed to
10. Obtain the ability to sign up for Richard's e-newsletter

If you are comfortable with your current setup you do not need this book.

---

[1] https://www.benzinga.com/analyst-ratings/analyst-color/20/03/15619056/where-does-the-market-go-from-here-keep-an-eye-on-this-crucial-s-p-500-level

[1] Every individual has his own interests in mind how does that apply to your portfolio?

INTRODUCTION

In the creation of this book, I have endeavored to keep the information as concise as possible; while providing you with knowledge that will help you be successful. Based on nearly 30 years of experience in the equity markets and almost 20 years of experience in the commodities markets my goal is to pass on some of my successful methods and behaviours.

Throughout my financial career I would hear a reoccurring statement coming from people on the street and investors alike," finally, my trading account has recovered to its' pre-tech wreck level." This screamed loud and clear to me that these people are not receiving sound advice. This is my chance to share with you some sound advice and offer you an opportunity for more if you wish.

The knowledge within these pages is based on my education and experience as follows;

Education:
Canadian Securities Institute

> I was licensed to trade <u>ALL</u> financial products publically offered in Canada (except Insurance) including futures and options products

University of Manitoba: Bachelor of Arts History and Economics

> I took all the macro-economic courses they offered at the time

Extensive Experience:

Actively trading within the equity markets since 1992 and the commodity markets since 2004.

Unique insight from working within the financial industry during the dotcom and real estate bubbles. Having worked extensively in the mining industry I have developed a thorough understanding of mining. The energy industry has become a favourite of mine due to my working and trading experience which also prompted me to allocate hundreds of hours researching it.

Some highlights from include:

- working at Canada's largest discount broker through the "tech wreck" 1999 to 2004
- during that time I watched million dollar accounts evaporate to nothing in months

- I recall buying 300 shares for a client and the next day he phoned in for a quote to discover that he had lost around C$100,000.
- Early in the '90s I bought Ballard Power Systems for C$5/share and subsequently sold them @ C$ 108/share.
- Almost to the day, my business partner and I correctly called a top in the stock market in July 2007.
- As result of my research our office (to the best of my knowledge) did not suffer any losses due to investing in Collateralized Debt Obligations (CDOs) before the 2008 financial crisis.

As I write in April 2020 I suspect most trading accounts have once again returned to valuations they had at the turn of the century + contributions – fees paid due to the Covid-19 selloff. The one account I am directing at the moment has not suffered any loss.

CHAPTER 1

Rules to trade by in Equity markets as well as the Commodity markets.

Rule #1

<u>Only trade with money that you are comfortable losing</u>

(if you lost the money would it adversely affect your standard of living?)☺

Anxiety over potential losses will likely result in poorer decision making and increase the probability of losing it.

Rule #2

<u>Document and set a realistic goal</u>

Ex. I have $10,000 and I would like to turn it into $20,000 within 5 years.

Keep track of your thoughts, decisions, and goals so that you can <u>accurately</u> review and learn from what you have done. As well as consult others as to their thoughts (if you don't mind sharing).

Rule #3

<u>Weigh the Risk</u>

You are determining whether or not the risk you accept with one investment is better than the risk profile of another investment.

Rule #4

<u>Research, Research, Research</u>

Become an expert on the market or stock you plan to trade.

Rule #5

<u>Emotion usually = losses</u>

It is very difficult not to get emotionally attached to an investment that you know have spent so much time with\on. But you must get in the habit of saying to yourself, "(*Investment*) does not care for me, it is just a tool for my use."

For example, a gold mining exploration company you have followed since it started operating[2], investing in it when the stock was mere pennies, you must be able to hit that sell button and say, "my hard work is paying off, I can live with that[3]."

Rule #6

<u>Anticipate</u>

Try as best you can to determine the stimuli that moves the price of your investment if applicable

For example if you create a laddered portfolio of <u>high</u> quality domestically denominated[4] bonds which you intend to hold to maturity the only concern you should have would be the integrity of the whole financial system.

If you intend to speculate on the price of Silver you will want to know which stimuli moves the price of silver.

I suggest looking at a significant price move on a chart and search for the news at that time. I like starting specifically with the product/company/nation and then widening the search.

For example you could find some moves in the price of corn are linked to drought expectations in corn growing regions.

Rule #7

<u>Sufficient Liquidity</u>

We all make mistakes. It is nice to know that if you make a mistake there is a high probability that you will be able to get some of your money back.

Also the greater the number of participants the more likely the stock or commodity is fairly priced.

---

[2]   Most brokers will only have access when the company sells shares on large stock exchanges
[3]   See Chapter 4 Buying and Chapter 5 Selling for more detail
[4]   No foreign exchange risk

2 rules of thumb

<u>The rule of 72 and "Who do you know?"</u>

The Rule of 72

- "If you invest money at a 10% return, you will double your money every 7.2 years. (72/10 = 7.2)
- If you invest at a 9% return, you will double your money every 8 years. (72/9 = 8)
- If you invest at an 8% return, you will double your money every 9 years. (72/8 = 9)
- If you invest at a 7% return, you will double your money every 10.2 years. (72/7 = 10.2)

The 25-year average annualized return for the S&P 500 from 1994 through 2018 was 8.52%. In other words, if you had invested in an index fund that tracks the S&P 500 in 1994 and you never withdrew the money, you would have average returns of 8.52% per year – any fees. At that rate, you should expect to double your money about every 8.45 years.[5]

The 25-year average annualized return for the S&P 500 from 1994 through 2018 gives you an excellent idea of what a medium risk investment could and should return.

Who do you know?

50% of startups fail within 5 years and 90% of them fail in total[6]. So if you do not know anyone involved or have some unique insight[7] into the situation. You have a 10% chance of picking a winner in the long run. Bottom line is a 10% probability of success is unacceptable, don't bother, there are other options. If you do know someone or have a unique insight then your probability of success should be higher.

---

[5]   https://www.thebalance.com/what-is-the-rule-of-72-how-can-it-help-you-double-your-money-453756
[6]   https://www.failory.com/blog/startup-failure-rate
[7]   For example, You worked in the industry or for the company

CHAPTER 2

Researching

Applicable to Equities and Commodities markets

When researching or forecasting there isn't any "right" way, I like to start globally and then narrow my focus. When looking at stocks I like to think of the respective stock market as a rough representation of the corporate wealth produced in that country. This phenomenon is easily visible this year (see appendix A); when participants in stocks around the world realized the extent of the pandemic they reacted, trying to gauge the damage coming to corporate profits.

So if we see a globe affecting event it is likely we will be able to buy things lower and\or protect the value of current holdings depending on the timing of this realization.

The next step which depends on your focus, may be to look at continents or countries or industries.

For example If you look at the energy industry you will find that renewable energy investments are soaring and investment in the Fossil Fuel industry have almost disappeared. You may have seen in the news that Tesla (the car/solar panel maker) is now the world's most valuable[8] car maker.

You can then continue the process looking at suitable companies and products.

------ Time Saver ------

We are typically all very busy with life and sometimes it is worthwhile to outsource some of the work we need done. I know that I would much rather write about economics and team humanity than read another balance sheet. So there can be a short cut to Rule #4.

Find as many different analysts that cover the company or product that you are focused on. If they are publically offering their opinion it is likely they have done their homework.

---

[8] https://www.msn.com/en-us/finance/companies/tesla-overtakes-toyota-as-the-world-e2-80-99s-most-valuable-automaker/ar-BB16dg0y

Most of the time you will find that there is a clear consensus; this will give you a good idea if the company or product fits your strategy.

****** When using this exception you must remember ******

- Most of the analysts have not left their desk to arrive at their decision,
- Most have not worked in the industry they are covering
- Their perspective is usually finite (limited to the industry)
- They have different goals than you do

You need to weigh all these factors in an effort to arrive at a decision.

Ok so let's continue the research process:

Common Questions for stocks:

1. Objective, What do you want? Ex. Dividends, Capital appreciation
2. Realism, how big is this company's target market? Ex. Global, regional, local
3. Efficiency, how are the company's finances? Ex. Income vs Costs
4. Leadership, what is the track records of the directors? Are they new or established
5. Need, are they part of a growing industry? Ex. fossil fuel co. vs renewable energy co.

Common Questions for both commodities and stocks:

1. Objective? Speculation or Hedging
2. Timeframe? Short-term (seconds, minutes, hours, days), Medium-term (months, 1-2 years), Long-term (2+ years)
3. Realism\Usefulness\Demand? What is used for? Will it continue to be used? Ex. Fossil fuels, Hogs, Currencies[9]
4. Charts: What is its' current price? Relative to recent prices (1-2 years), relative to historical prices (2+ years), adjusted for inflation (assume 3%)[10] ? 5 and 10 year averages? How do they **compare**? How strong is the relationship to other commodities? Ex. US treasuries and the Equity markets

Once you have determined your objective and timeframe you can really start to focus on products that will satisfy your needs.

Let's look at a couple of equity research examples:

- Objective: Find 5 acceptable dividend stocks to be held for 2+ years
- Size: Preferably large, with national and/or international operations
- Finances: Annual profits that justify the dividend?

---

[9] The central theme of my next book
[10] https://inflationdata.com/articles/charts/decade-inflation-chart/

- Burn rate: Annual profits that justify the dividend? Industry growing? Declining? Mature?
- Leadership: Proven and steady? Shaky? Unknown?
- Usefulness: We are actively changing the way we live; part of a growing industry or a declining one?
- High quality dividends: 4-5% is achievable in Canada

And

- Objective: Build a bond ladder[11] with a 25 year timeframe.
- Size: National Government issue or select AAA rated Corporate offerings
- Finances: National macro-outlook if one exists, political stability
- Burn rate: Demographics
- Usefulness: Is the company growing? Is the product line desirable?
- Leadership: Primarily political stability
- Dividend: Interest rates may determine your focus, ex. many nations currently have 0-1% yields on their long term bonds, it may be worth considering 1-3% high quality corporate GIC 's.

At this highly unique and uncertain time let's run through the process for each example. Please be aware that the current prices you see are the result of countless factors including manipulation[12]; the following are the dominant issues of the day.

Global

Covid-19 has mutated already several times and according to experts[13] this likely will not cause effectiveness issues if a vaccine is found. Based on this information I would assume as market participants have, that a vaccine will be found, whether that occurs in 2020 is another story. Soaring infection rates[14] and decreasing death rates coupled with lockdown frustration are increasing the probability that we will have to learn to live [15] with the presence of Covid-19. Given the economic structure in the majority of nations; infection rates will continue to soar as workers around the world return to work having weighed the risks of dying against little or no income.[16]

The shift to renewable energy continues in earnest we should see the demand for oil start to fall significantly within 4-5 years; affecting the viability of oil producers.

---

[11] https://www.investopedia.com/terms/b/bondladder.asp
[12] https://www.cnbc.com/2020/07/20/bernanke-and-yellen-say-the-fed-needs-to-find-out-why-the-market-broke-down-in-march.html
[13] https://www.healthline.com/health-news/what-to-know-about-mutation-and-covid-19#Just-how-long-will-immunity-last?
[14] https://www.worldometers.info/coronavirus/
[15] https://www.forbes.com/sites/toddhixon/2020/03/12/get-ready-to-live-with-covid-19/#339f4e334782
      https://medicalxpress.com/news/2020-06-covid--1.html
[16] https://www.newschannel5.com/news/advocate-frustrated-as-covid-19-cases-soar-in-the-hispanic-community

National

Narrowing our focus, the status of Chinese US[17] trade was having an effect on prices and sentiment. Both parties need each other and the wealth that relationship creates. A deal of some kind will occur, it looks to me like the participants in the stock markets feel the same way therefore a deal is mostly priced in already and once done, the market is likely to sell off some and then return to business as usual.

- US - Civil unrest and the fact that US troops[18] are being used against Americans is worrisome.
- US -It is advisable that due to a clear lack of leadership in the US you may want to delay any investment there until there is a return to competent leadership hopefully in 2021.
- Canada-Steady leadership, sadly Canada is blessed and cursed with an abundance of natural resources; due to a lack of ingenuity and political will; Canada will underperform its economic potential. Despite steady stream of scandals the investment environment within Canada is safe.
- China-Leadership there appears to be quite competent however it also oppressive and to be avoided.
- Japan-Leadership looks steady[19]a rise in military spending seems to be prudent given the regional politics and an absence of US leadership; however 0% interest rates and neutral/ bearish outlook[20] has me thinking there are better opportunities
- Australia[21] and New Zealand[22]-Good leadership and an isolation advantage in fighting Covid-19 give us a positive view, particularly New Zealand.
- Euro Zone-Mostly competent leadership especially in Germany[23].
- UK- Questionable leadership that is hamstrung trying to deliver Brexit[24] makes for a volatile environment (easily seen in the fluctuations of the pound[25])
- Switzerland[26]-Steady leadership, good position, and positive history.
- Africa – Can be looked at on a case by case basis, there are good opportunities but the overall risk starts higher making them more difficult to find
- Latin America – Also can be looked at on a case by case basis, there are good opportunities but the overall risk starts higher making them more difficult to find

---

[17] https://www.bloomberg.com/news/articles/2020-07-01/u-s-readies-global-sanctions-on-china-over-xinjiang-abuses

[18] https://thehill.com/homenews/state-watch/509214-mayors-urge-congress-to-pass-legislation-against-deployment-of-federal

[19] https://thediplomat.com/2015/03/is-japans-militarization-normal/

[20] https://www.focus-economics.com/countries/japanhttps://www.japanpolicyforum.jp/blog/pt20200116131126.html

[21] https://www.focus-economics.com/countries/australia

[22] https://www.focus-economics.com/countries/new-zealand

[23] https://www.focus-economics.com/countries/germany

[24] https://www.irishtimes.com/life-and-style/abroad/anti-irish-sentiment-in-britain-i-feel-like-i-am-back-in-the-1980s-1.3992131

[25] See Appendix B

[26] https://www.focus-economics.com/countries/switzerland

Summarizing our stock search, we should focus our search in Switzerland, New Zealand/Australia, and the Euro-zone particularly Germany. In the event that you do not want exposure to currency risk most nations should be ok; it is likely the US will eventually sort out some of its many problems; you will just have to stomach the irritating manner in which this is accomplished. Despite disappointing leadership in Canada and the UK, long term investment is still considered safe.

The same research can be used to choose the various bonds required in the bond ladder.

You can use this site[27] to find some appropriate bonds, beware the number of options can be overwhelming.

---

[27] https://markets.businessinsider.com/bonds?op=1

Investment plan   Date _____

Account name   _____

Funding account   lump sum/monthly contribution

How much am I ok loosing?   _____

Risk profile?   Low/medium/high

Time Frame   short/medium/long

Investment vehicles?   stocks/mutual funds/bonds/etf/options/futures

Preferred industries if any   _____

Sub-industries?   _____

Preferred vehicles if any   _____

Notes

Goal   _____

Narrowing the Focus, Stocks

Goal _____ Date _____

Symbol	Name	Last	years in biz, Analysts Buy/Sell/Hold	Industry	Div%
_____	___	___	_____	_____	__
_____	___	___	_____	_____	__
_____	___	___	_____	_____	__
_____	___	___	_____	_____	__
_____	___	___	_____	_____	__
_____	___	___	_____	_____	__
_____	___	___	_____	_____	__
_____	___	___	_____	_____	__

Symbol	Name	Last	years in biz, Analysts Buy/Sell/Hold	Industry	Div%
_____	___	___	_____	_____	__
_____	___	___	_____	_____	__
_____	___	___	_____	_____	__
_____	___	___	_____	_____	__
_____	___	___	_____	_____	__
_____	___	___	_____	_____	__

There are many https://www.zacks.com/screening/stock-screener?icid=stocks-stocks-nav_tracking-zcom-main_menu_wrapper-stock_screener

https://ca.investing.com/stock-screener/?sp=country::6|sector::a|industry::a|equityType::a|yield_us::2.07,31.04|qquickrati_us::0,144.9%3Cyield_us;1

https://www.marketbeat.com/stocks/OTCMKTS/SWDBY/price-target/

Research on _____ Date: _____

Last: _____

Objective:	Speculation	-	Dividends	- Growth	-	Safety	-	Hedge
Time Frame:	Short	-	Medium (months – 2 years)		-	Long (2 + years)		
Size:	Local	-	Regional	- Global	-			N/A
Finances:	Good	-	Questionable	- Bad	-	not sure		N/A
Burn rate:	Fast	-	Slow	- estimate when refinancing required ___ years-				N/A
Leadership:	Appears to competent	-	Appears Incompetent		-	Not sure	-	N/A
Liquidity:	Concerning	-	Not a concern					N/A
Lifespan:	Growing	-	Declining	- Passively Monitor	-	Actively monitor	-	N/A
Why? _____								N/A
Dividend?:	Yes - No		amount_____	yield _____		Quarterly	Annual	N/A
Expected Volatility:	High	-	Medium	- Low				N/A

Opinion _____ Bullish - Bearish - Neutral Why _____

Opinion _____ Bullish - Bearish - Neutral Why _____

Opinion _____ Bullish - Bearish - Neutral Why _____

Opinion _____ Bullish - Bearish - Neutral Why _____

Charts (print and attach) Summary

Buy Zone _____ N/A

Sell Zone _____ N/A

RETIREMENT PLAN CURRENT AGE 60

CANADA

Investment plan

Date July 18/20

Account name
RETIREMENT

Funding account
(lump sum/monthly contribution $ 300,000

How much am I ok loosing?

Risk profile?
(Low/medium)high

Time Frame
short/medium/(long)

Investment vehicles?
(stocks/mutual funds/bonds/etf/options/futures

Preferred industries if any
NO EXPOSURE to OIL INDUSTRY

Sub-industries?
No Preference

Preferred vehicles if any
STOCKS OR BONDS

Notes
AVG LIFE EXPECTANCY IN CANADA is 82.5 YEARS

RETIREMENT PlAN CANADA   No Fossil Fuel stock

Narrowing the Focus, Stocks

YIELD
Goal 6% ↑ Date Jul 18/20

C#

Symbol Name	Last	years in biz,	Analysts Buy/Sell/Hold	Industry	Div%
BNS	56.58	188		BANK	
EIF	26.94	15+		AVIATION	8.46
SLF pa	22.39	150+		FINANCIAL	
RSI	4.82	135		FOOD	7.47
RUS	17.30	100+		STEEL	6.63
CHS.u	9.66	17		RETIREMENT HOUSING	6.34
CM	93.54	59		BANK	6.24
BMO	74.60	203		BANK	5.68

(left margin note: erred A / preferred A)

Symbol Name	Last	years in biz,	Analysts Buy/Sell/Hold	Industry	Div%
BCE	57.69	37		TELECOM	5.28
RY	95.91	156		BANK	4.51

(Index)

Research on <u>S&P 500</u> Date: <u>July 20/20</u>

Last: <u>3246</u>

Objective:	Speculation - Dividends - Growth - Safety - (Hedge)	**DETERMINE**
Time Frame:	Short - (Medium (months – 2 years)) - Long (2 + years)	**IF NECESSARY**
Size:	Local - Regional - (Global) -	N/A
Finances:	Good - Questionable - Bad - not sure	(N/A)
Burn rate:	Fast - Slow - estimate when refinancing required ___ years -	(N/A)
Leadership:	Appears to competent - Appears Incompetent - Not sure -	(N/A)
Liquidity:	Concerning - Not a concern	(N/A)
Lifespan:	Growing - Declining - Passively Monitor - Actively monitor -	(N/A)
Why?	<u>Protect Portfolio / DELAY BUYING</u>	N/A
Dividend?:	Yes - No amount ____ yield ____ Quarterly Annual	(N/A)
Expected Volatility:	(High) - Medium - Low	N/A

Opinion <u>WEBSITE 1</u> Bullish - Bearish - (Neutral) Why <u>COVID EFFECTS ON EARNING</u>

Opinion <u>WEBSITE 2</u> Bullish - (Bearish) - Neutral Why <u>Giting SAME Action As LATE 2019</u>

Opinion _____ Bullish - Bearish - Neutral Why _____

Opinion _____ Bullish - Bearish - Neutral Why _____

Opinion _____ Bullish - Bearish - Neutral Why _____

How MUCH OF APRIL – MID-JUNE RALLY IS DUE to Assumption
" THAT A VACCINE will be FOUND."?

As OF Jul 14/20 TRADE TALKS WITH CHINA ARE CANCELLED

Charts (print and attach summary

Civil UNREST INN THE US. is LIKELY to GET <u>WORSE</u>

Sell Zone _____ N/A

WHy WOULD STOCKS GO UP ?

WELL IF A VACCINE IS FOUND – BUT How MUCH OF THAT is
PRICED IN ?

Lots of TALK, STILL NO VACCINE

(MSFT)

Research on M<u>ICROSOFT</u>   Date: J<u>ul 18/20</u>

Last: <u>202.88</u> USD

Objective: Speculation - Dividends - (Growth) - Safety - Hedge

Time Frame: Short   -   Medium (months – 2 years) - Long (2 + years)

Size: Local -   Regional   -   (Global) -   N/A

Finances: (Good)   Questionable -   Bad - not sure   N/A

Burn rate: Fast - Slow - estimate when refinancing required ___ years -   (N/A)

Leadership: Appears to competent - Appears Incompetent - Not sure -   N/A

Liquidity: Concerning   - (Not a concern)   CURRENTLY   N/A

Lifespan: (Growing)   -   Declining - Passively Monitor - Actively monitor - N/A

Why? <u>CONTINUES to DELIVER USEFUL SOFTWARE</u> N/A

Dividend?: (Yes) - No   amount 1.01 % yield _____ (Quarterly)   Annual   N/A

Expected Volatility: High   - (Medium) - Low   N/A

Opinion WEBSITE 1   (Bullish) - Bearish - Neutral Why NEWTECH, COVID REVENUE BOOSTED
Opinion WEBSITE 2   Bullish - Bearish - (Neutral) Why _____
Opinion WEBSITE 3   (Bullish) - Bearish - Neutral Why _____
Opinion WEBSITE 4   (Bullish) - Bearish - Neutral Why _____
Opinion _____   Bullish - Bearish - Neutral Why _____

OUTLOOK FOR NEAR TERM OVERALL MARKET IS BEARISH
WE CAN WAIT, HOWEVER PRICE ACTION SHOULD BE
FOLLOWED CLOSELY AS EARNINGS WERE POSITIVELY AFFECTED
BY COVID LOCKDOWNS

Charts (print and attach) Summary

Buy Zone 130, 170, OR 190
Sell Zone IF IT BREAKS 130' RE-EVALUATE (QUICKLY)

(TSLA)

Research on _TESLA_   Date: _Jul 18/20_

Last: _1500.84_

Objective: Speculation - Dividends - (Growth) - Safety - Hedge

Time Frame: Short   -   Medium (months – 2 years) - (Long (2 + years))

Size: Local -   Regional   -   (Global)   N/A

Finances: Good -   Questionable   -   Bad - (not sure)   N/A

Burn rate: Fast - Slow - estimate when refinancing required ___ years - (N/A)

Leadership: (Appears to competent) - Appears Incompetent - Not sure -   N/A

Liquidity: (Concerning) - Not a concern   N/A

Lifespan: (Growing)   - Declining   - Passively Monitor - Actively monitor - N/A

Why? _INDUSTRY LEADER IN GROWING INDUSTRY_

Dividend?: Yes - (No)   amount _____ yield _____   Quarterly   Annual N/A

Expected Volatility: (High) - Medium - Low   N/A

Opinion _WEBSITE 1_   Bullish - Bearish - (Neutral) Why _HOLD_

Opinion _WEBSITE 2_   Bullish - Bearish - (Neutral) Why _Buy to Hold_

Opinion _WEBSITE 3_   Bullish - Bearish - (Neutral) Why _HOLD_

Opinion _WEBSITE 4_   Bullish - Bearish - (Neutral) Why _Hold_

Opinion _____   Bullish - Bearish - Neutral Why _____

VOLATILITY MAKES ENTRY LEVELS A TOUGH CALL
ON A PULLBACK YOU COULD WATCH FOR THE PRICE TO
LEVEL OUT ON HEAVY VOLUME

Charts (print and attach) Summary _____

Buy Zone _____   N/A

Sell Zone _____   N/A

CHAPTER 3

Risk and Perspective

Risk

It is extremely important that your risk tolerance matches the risk you accept. I can't tell you how many times I've seen retirees (who do not want high risk) with high risk tech stocks. Ignore GREED it will only get you into trouble, try to think of money manipulation as a tool you would like to use to accomplish a goal.

Low risk – instruments whose value is highly probable to increase slowly over the long term; usually securities that are tied to a physical asset or guaranteed such as bonds, GIC's, t-bills, preferred shares. They are also usually top of the list of creditors to paid out first in the event of bankruptcy.

Medium risk – instruments whose value fluctuations lie between the extremes Low and High risk. So usually companies that are in the mature stage of the business model.

High risk – Can be any instruments whose pricing has the power to increase or decrease significantly in a short time frame.

"Learn to smell a rat! If it seems too good to be true it likely is."

For example during an interview I had with a CDO[28] salesman I realized that there was something very wrong with CDO's. At the time US treasuries (a high quality bond that carried a AAA rating) were yielding around 3% the salesman's CDO's yielded 6 or 7% and carried AAA rating. I had one question for him, "Why are your securities yielding twice what the market for AAA securities is yielding?"

His answer had something to do with a little black box, which I quickly translated into, "he didn't know" and therefore I thanked him for his time and shared the experience with the rest of the office. Several months later the "Financial Crisis"[29] started by sub-prime lending and was exacerbated by CDO's.

---

[28]   Collateralized Debt Obligation, a Mortgage Backed Security (MBS) is a CDO

[29]   https://en.wikipedia.org/wiki/Subprime_mortgage_crisis see 2nd paragraph

Use widely known benchmarks to compare instruments against, this might seem to be common sense but greed can blind us.

Perspective

Try to get as many opinions as possible, professional, non-professional, industry workers, and interested parties.

News Outlets are a great source of perspectives

In March 2004 I became aware of the Madrid train bombings before they were reported in North America. My Twitter feed went crazy alerting me to the fact that something was going on at which point I was able to search Spanish papers online to confirm and adjust my trading strategy.

At the time it was my job to monitor the news and provide the best information that I could for my clients whose goals spanned the entire risk spectrum. For many of you; thorough research will eliminate the need to monitor geopolitics so closely.

I got lucky, it just so happened I was looking at my Twitter feed at the time; there are couple of issues that I would like to point out here:

1. Do your best to have relevant news collected for you as fast as it is generated if possible, ex. Twitter/Social media (discussed in more detail below)
2. Confirm to the best your ability the depth of truth by gathering as many perspectives as possible.
3. Local news outlets – do your best to get a story from the location of the event, ex. A Spanish or Madrid paper for an event in Spain, a Japanese or Tokyo paper for an event in Japan etc.

It is very important that you recognize that "Fake News" does exist and you can protect yourself by using multiple sources.

Most news platforms ask you when you join what content you would prefer to see, allowing to focus your attention as you wish.

Here is a sample source list:

www.BBC.com

A European perspective and a good place to start due to their extensive news gathering network.

www.aljazeera.com

an Arabic perspective that also has extensive network.

<u>www.thepaperboy.com</u>

a gateway to many local papers, you may have to broaden your search to a regional paper to find an English version.

It is <u>very important</u> to accept that every news outlet has bias of some type and reading the same story from several different perspectives can give you a better understanding what is actually happening. It also has the added bonus of making you less susceptible to "fake news".

<u>People's perspectives</u>

Whoever you talk to **always** bear in mind they have a personal agenda and also be aware that the person you are talking to may not be aware of what it is. A few ex. :

- A person working within the financial industry will benefit from your participation either directly or indirectly.
- A person giving you a stock tip may be trying to get out of a low liquidity stock
- They work for the company they are promoting
- They could be having a bad day and intentionally give you bad information
- They make an honest mistake
- To name a few

Whether or not that is person is aware of their bias, is not as important as your awareness of the possibility.

PS – If someone quotes FOX news, you should ask them to clarify, "don't you mean the Comedy Network?"

CHAPTER 4

Buying

Depending on your goal, you may not be too concerned with your entry price. For example if you are creating a bond ladder with high quality bonds and plan to hold them to maturity or you have constructed a dividend portfolio and some of the stocks do not move very much.

But in a lot of cases your entry point into the market can be the difference between success and failure; therefore here are few tips.

<u>Charts Charts and more Charts</u>

Obtain the longest dated chart you can, this will show you of how the other participants have been pricing in the past. Bear in mind that the chart is showing you how participants valued the instrument using the publically available information at the time.

Tempting as it might be, I don't recommend you skip doing the research; because you may uncover valuable information in the process. For example, my business partner at the time and I were researching a Real Estate Investment Trust for our dividend seeking clients, and they had just announced that they were going make a big investment, having just reviewed their latest balance sheet we knew that they did not have the cash to make such a purchase and they would have to sell more company equity to raise the cash. Sure enough a few days later they announced they were diluting the stock some more and we were able to buy it cheaper.

Don't be in a hurry, feel free to place buy orders below the current price and adjust if need be.

Royal Bank (RY) and Johnson and Johnson (JNJ)[30] provide us with good sets of data in which to form a buying decision. Outside of major[31] events both stocks tend pull back around 10% after a good up trend.

---

[30]   Charts at the end of the chapter
[31]   The tech wreck 2000, 2001 – the financial crisis 2008, 2009 – the Covid correction 2020, 20??

Corn provides a fantastic commodity example of how you could time your buying, It has a long-term trading range of $ US 2-5 /bushel that is rarely breeched. You can easily see that buying Corn at $5 /bushel is high risk compared to buying it between $ 2-3 /bushel. Buying at either price can still make sense, the point is, if you are patient you can choose to wait for a lower risk,/higher probability win.

Plan your entry and exit points[32]

JNJ – Johnson and Johson

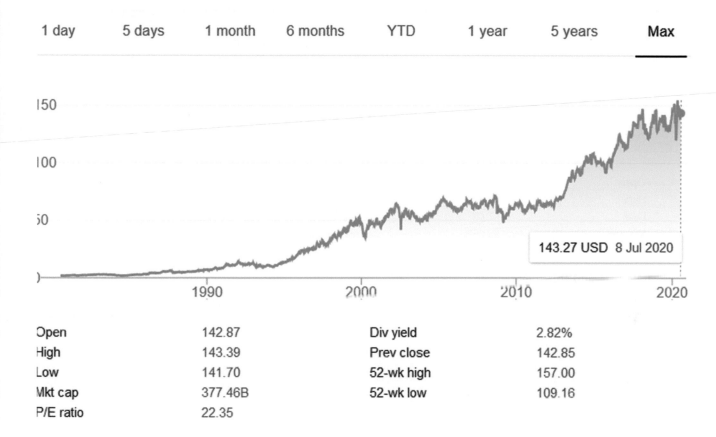

| 1 day | 5 days | 1 month | 6 months | YTD | 1 year | 5 years | **Max** |

143.27 USD 8 Jul 2020

Open	142.87	Div yield	2.82%
High	143.39	Prev close	142.85
Low	141.70	52-wk high	157.00
Mkt cap	377.46B	52-wk low	109.16
P/E ratio	22.35		

---

[32] When the exit price is predetermined (for ex.bonds) write it down in your plan anyway

RY – Royal Bank of Canada in US

68.48 USD +1.33 (1.98%) ↑
Closed: Jul. 10, 4:00 p.m. EDT · Disclaimer
After hours 68.48 0.00 (0.00%)

| 1 day | 5 days | 1 month | 6 months | YTD | 1 year | 5 years | **Max** |

68.48 USD 10 Jul 2020

Open	67.03	Div yield	4.59%
High	68.51	Prev close	67.15
Low	67.03	52-wk high	82.74
Mkt cap	98.05B	52-wk low	49.55

RY - Royal Bank of Canada in Canada

93.08 CAD +1.81 (1.98%) ↑
Jul. 10, 4:00 p.m. EDT · Disclaimer

| 1 day | 5 days | 1 month | 6 months | YTD | 1 year | 5 years | **Max** |

93.08 CAD 10 Jul 2020

Open	91.24	Div yield	4.64%
High	93.16	Prev close	91.27
Low	91.24	52-wk high	109.68
Mkt cap	132.49B	52-wk low	72.00
P/E ratio	11.92		

CHAPTER 5

Selling

Please remember everyone's personal situation is different; for ex. the top 10% of wealth holders may not care if they lose $ 100,000.00 on an investment but the other 90% of us would find such a loss to be an unwelcome setback. So when it comes to selling I have 2 methods I employ that I would like to share with you:

1. Double it! - (usually for high risk stocks) when selling stock that has either doubled in price or more

For example,

I frequently buy thousands of shares of gold or mineral exploration companies at less than $C 0.50 per share. If the price doubles I will sell half and remove my initial investment eliminating risk of loss. Thereafter I'll continue selling half the remaining stock with each significant price increase (could be tripled or more). The situation usually determines your reaction but I find removing my initial investment makes it much easier to be objective and read movements in the stock.

This seems to be common practice with traders in penny stocks, for example a company goes public @ $ 0.25 it is very likely that it will find significant selling pressure around the $0.50 mark.

2. Move on - outright sell when your target has been achieved or place a trailing stop loss order underneath the current price.

The trick with stop orders is not to get caught in a temporary pullback as the price ebb and flows higher. Once again charts can help us with determining a suitable stop and exit; you can study the depth of the historical pullbacks to determine these levels.

For example, you have a stock that has increased in price to the point where you would sell it, however analysts are calling for it to appreciate another 20%. Thus far daily pullbacks have not exceeded 2% so you place your stop just below that. The result being that you get stopped out and the stock then proceeds to increase the 20% the analysts predicted.

Be diligent when selling because the psychology of greed can get you!. You must try not to have seller's remorse. Remember that;

1. your research and hard work paid off
2. there will always be other opportunities.

One of the great features of this game is that no one method will work for everyone. The best advice I can give you is be happy with success, be methodical if you feel that you are repeatedly selling too early examine your documented process for clues as to how to improve.

CHAPTER 6

Introduction to the Next Level

***** WARNING *****

You must **FULLY** understand how Options products work before trading them. I highly recommend that you talk to and use a licensed professional when starting.

http://www.cboe.com/education/

https://www.cmegroup.com/education.html

https://www.optionseducation.org/theoptionseducationcenter/occ-learning

https://www.eurexchange.com/exchange-en/resources/education

If you would like to take full advantage of all aspects of this game you need to learn how options work and in doing so you will find that Futures are very similar. Once you take that step and learn how they work, literally a whole new world will be before you! That is a story for another day.

Today I am here to make you aware that this world exists, options and futures can be as safe as insurance and more dangerous than going to a casino.

As an ex. You can buy term insurance for your portfolio to protect it against a decline in value – in industry talk you would buy puts on the appropriate index (S&P 500 or Nasdaq or Nikkei).

I will be covering more complex strategies within my e-newsletter.

CHAPTER 7

Commodities Summary

***** WARNING *****

Again, you must **FULLY** understand how Futures and Options products work before trading them. I highly recommend that you talk to and use a licensed professional when starting.

Personally my focus has turned largely to the commodities markets mainly because:

1. Flexibility/Structure - they allow you the same opportunity to profit from declines in a commodities price as a price increase.
2. Optics – you can easily access supply/demand information or other market moving stimuli and often from different sources

<u>Flexibility/Structure</u>

For Example; if you do not have a position; you can sell a corn contract just the same as you would buy one even though you don't own one.

Numerically it looks like this;

Your account positions starts at 0 (no position)

You can sell some corn and have a position of -1 just as easily as you can have a positive position +1.

I know it takes a little getting used to.

Overall I prefer the grain complex, the "softs", and metal markets for the following reasons:

- Demand - as long as they are edible demand will remain
- Volatility – they have a typical trading range, only a major disaster would change this
- Optics – you can easily access information on planting progress and weather forecasts are readily available

- Math – Market participants are pretty much forced to accept the economics of supply/demand because they are so visible, (satellites/storage bins)
- "Softs" have many of the same traits as the grain markets but are more luxuries than staples
- Gold, Silver, and Copper have stood the test of time and human perception that they hold value will not change anytime soon.

Optics

The grain markets are largely driven by supply and demand, and you can literally see (via satellite) how much corn, wheat, and soybeans have been planted. At each step of the production process there are several checks and balances:

- Elevators buying the grain
- Rail companies picking up the grain
- Shippers moving the grain to foreign buyers

At each step the results of the transaction are known.

The probability of a participant cheating is not zero however it is unlikely for fear of being labeled a cheater and evicted from the market.

Here are a few underlying reasons why I tend to avoid some markets.

- The Fossil fuel complex is running on borrowed time. Demand will collapse as alternatives that provide the same benefits without most if not all of the negative aspects, will replace it.
- Currency markets will eventually collapse or convert to the next medium[33]
- Red meat is a highly inefficient form of protein, the cattle market in particular
- Stock and Bond markets are both heavily manipulated[34], the structure of the stock market makes it very difficult to short singular stocks making the price discovery mechanism one sided; it has become common practice for central banks to interfere/intervene.[35]

---

[33] Subject of my next book

[34] https://www.forbes.com/sites/investor/2019/04/17/the-fed-continues-to-manipulate-the-markets/#47aa7d0427df

[35] https://www.forbes.com/sites/investor/2019/10/09/qt-is-dead-qe-lives-what-the-feds-handbrake-turn-means/#12570dad3318

CHAPTER 8

Corn (Symbol ZC)

Longevity! Corn has been with us since we started farming millennia ago.

We can see on the monthly[36] that over the past 30 years the price of corn rarely exceeded $US 4.50 / bu. has not fell below $US 3.00 / bu. for very long in the last 15 years or below $US 2.00 / bu. in the last 30 years perhaps longer.

If you look at the trading action you can see that participants are very aware of the above traits, with significant buying near $US 3.00 /bu. and the bearish fundamentals encouraging significant selling at the $US 4.00 / bu.

Researching today's Corn market we find that several stimuli indicates significant bearish pressure on prices[37]:

- High corn stocks
- Record acres planted
- Harvest expectations are high

Logically based on that information you might feel that buying corn right now is a high risk proposition. Again consulting that monthly chart[38] we can see that the price of corn has not been lower that $US 1.74/ bu in 30 years and has not traded lower than $US 3.00/ bu since September 2009. Conversely the price of corn frequently exceeds $US 4.00 / bu. and occasionally $US 5.50 / bu. and been as high as $US 8.43 ¾ / bu.

So assuming that the corn plant will continue to be edible, there is a high probability that the price of corn will not fall below $US 2.00/bu. Based on this information I feel there is serious risk in selling (going short) corn right now and very limited risk in buying (going long).

---

[36]   Page 29

[37]   https://seekingalpha.com/article/4271749-corn-prices-on-move-all-supply-and-demand

[38]   Page ??

In this case depending on the depth of your pockets I would consider going long by either:

- buying some Dec corn or Mar 21 corn calls (here there is a time limit but if you can't afford the losses in the worst case scenario it's an option)[39]
- or Dec or Mar 21 futures outright (you can always roll out to another expiry if needed)

Looking closer at that monthly chart if you bought 1 contract of corn @ $US 3.50 / bu and sold it $US 0.25 higher and did that repeatedly you would make roughly $US 1200.00 each time over 5 years. When I see stuff like this I feel that my money is much safer in the commodity market at the whim of the weather than the clowns manipulating stocks around the world.

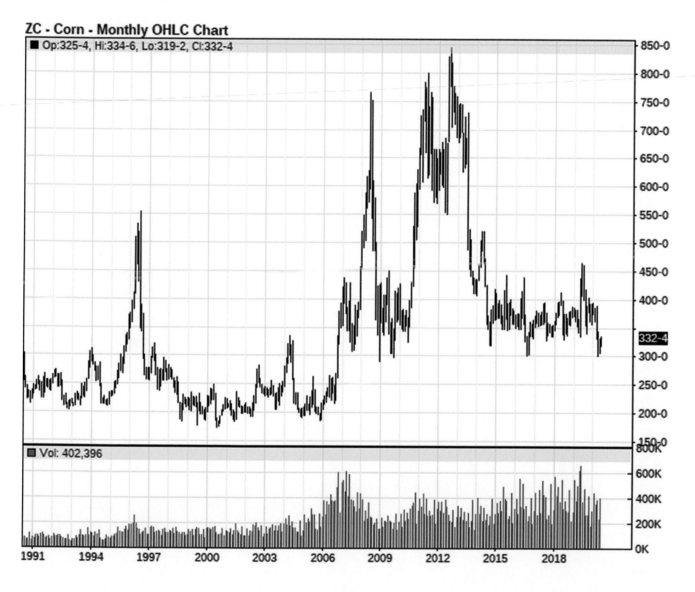

ZC - Corn - Monthly OHLC Chart
Op:325-4, Hi:334-6, Lo:319-2, Cl:332-4

---

[39]   Pun intended

Research on *Corn*   Date: *Jul 18/20*

Last: *331 1/4*

Objective: ~~Speculation~~ - Dividends - Growth - Safety - Hedge

Time Frame: ~~Short~~   -   Medium (months – 2 years) -   Long (2 + years)

Size: Local -   Regional   -   ~~Global~~ -   N/A

Finances: Good -   Questionable -   Bad - not sure   ~~N/A~~

Burn rate: Fast - Slow - estimate when refinancing required ___ years -   ~~N/A~~

Leadership: Appears to competent - Appears Incompetent - Not sure -   ~~N/A~~

Liquidity: Concerning   -   Not a concern   ~~N/A~~

Lifespan: Growing   -   Declining   - Passively Monitor - Actively monitor   ~~N/A~~

Why? _____   ~~N/A~~

Dividend?: Yes - ~~No~~   amount _____ yield _____   Quarterly   Annual   ~~N/A~~

N/A

Expected Volatility: High - ~~Medium~~ - Low

Opinion *WEBSITE 1*   Bullish - ~~Bearish~~ - Neutral   Why *Big Supply*

Opinion *WEBSITE 2*   Bullish - ~~Bearish~~ - Neutral   Why *No Planting Problem*

Opinion *WEBSITE 3*   Bullish - ~~Bearish~~ - Neutral   Why *No Weather Issues Yet*

Opinion _____   Bullish - Bearish - Neutral   Why _____

Opinion _____   Bullish - Bearish - Neutral   Why _____

Charts (print and attach) Summary

Buy Zone *SEE CHART A*

Sell Zone _____   N/A

CHAPTER 9

Wheat (Symbol ZW)

Longevity! Wheat has also been with us for millennia.

The basic thinking we used with the corn market can be applied here.

Consulting (see below) our monthly wheat chart wheat last traded @ $US 4.79 ½ / bu

We can see that over the past 30 years the price of wheat does not fall below $US 3.00 / bu. for very long and has not fallen below $US 2.30 / bu.

Conversely the price of wheat frequently exceeds $US 5.00 / bu. and occasionally $US 7.00 / bu. and been as high as $US 13.34 ½ / bu.

So again if you have the pockets and patience there is a very high probability that buying wheat low around $US 4.00 / bu. will likely be profitable if you are looking for something with a higher risk/reward profile.

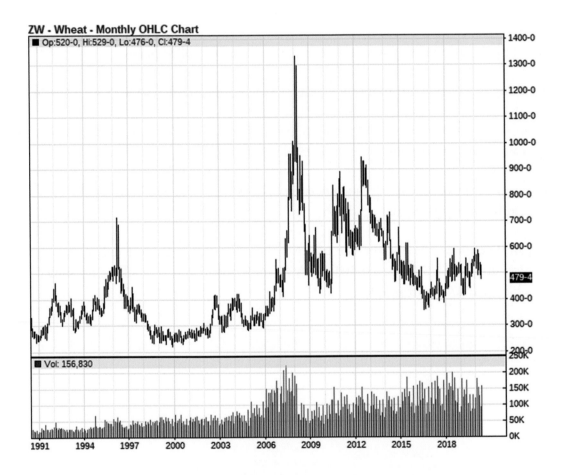

ZW - Wheat - Monthly OHLC Chart
Op:520-0, Hi:529-0, Lo:476-0, Cl:479-4

Research on __Wheat (ZW)__ Date: __July 20/20__

Last: __520 ¼__

Objective: (Speculation) - Dividends - Growth - Safety - Hedge

Time Frame: (Short) - (Medium (months) 2 years) - Long (2 + years)

Size: Local - Regional - (Global) - N/A

Finances: Good - Questionable - Bad - not sure (N/A)

Burn rate: Fast - Slow - estimate when refinancing required ___ years - (N/A)

Leadership: Appears to competent - Appears Incompetent - Not sure - (N/A)

Liquidity: Concerning - (Not a concern) - N/A

Lifespan: Growing - Declining - Passively Monitor - Actively monitor - (N/A)

Why? _____ (N/A)

Dividend?: Yes - No   amount ____ yield ____ Quarterly   Annual (N/A)

Expected Volatility: High - (Medium) - Low   N/A

Opinion __WEBSITE 1__   (LEANING) Bullish - Bearish - (Neutral) Why __WHEAT EXPORTS__ (THROUGH July 9) Above Expectati

Opinion __WEBSITE 2__   (Bullish) - Bearish - Neutral Why __ENDING STOCKS LOWER__

Opinion __WEBSITE 3__   (Bullish) - Bearish - Neutral Why __LOW PROTEIN LEVELS__

Opinion _____   Bullish - Bearish - Neutral Why __U.S. HARD RED WINTER WHEAT__

Opinion _____   Bullish - Bearish - Neutral Why _____

Charts (print and (attach) Summary

Buy Zone _____   N/A

Sell Zone _____   N/A

CHAPTER 10

Research on Automated Trading (Commodities and Stocks)

Using computers to try to profit from trading stocks faster is a waste of time, even if you had the capital and the will you would be entering the crowded market of HFTs[40] splitting the finite pie of profits.

It may be worth investing in an A.I. Artificial Intelligence that runs on algorithms in either stocks or commodities; one that has shown consistent profit even in significant downturns and has proven long term positive results.

In the commodity markets the quality of equal opportunity for price discovery and the addition of a time component to the structure of the market that makes the commodity markets a more unbiased game. So over the last couple of years I tried to use automated commodity trading to follow and profit from the ebb and flows of a market with limited success; given the potential rewards I will continue to do so.

It is likely that there are some great automated commodity trading programs out there, if you think you have found one, I encourage you to practice due diligence.

---

40   http://www.cnbc.com/2014/04/03/high-frequency-traders-cant-front-run-anyonecommentary.html

CHAPTER 11

Overall Summary

Even though I am no longer officially in the financial industry and have very limited contact with new people, due to the virus and my social habits; this conversation still happens roughly once per month.

Upon learning that I used to be a commodity broker (random person) excitedly asks in relation to stocks,

"what are you buying right now?" and depending on the timing, I reply,

"I am currently selling everything." Or "I have all my money in short term GIC's at the moment." Or

"I'm in cash waiting for a significant pull back."

Almost always this shuts down the conversation, very rarely does anyone ask why?

There is a good reason for this, so I don't take it personally. Part of the reason is a large portion of the world's wealth is stored here and most people knowingly or not have an interest in seeing it go higher. People have become so sensitive to market fluctuations it's become politically advantageous to support the pyramid by using the resources[41] of future generations. Any consideration of a downturn is an unpleasant thought at best.

I have included my research on the S&P1 at this point in time, to summarize the American's have already borrowed $US 5 Trillion[42] to support the economy and the stock market. How much more can they borrow before the lenders start to demand higher interest rates? We shall see, one huge advantage that the US has over all other nations at the moment, is that the US dollar is used and accepted right around the world. What happens if that changes? China is promising to release its crypto currency the E-Yuan[43].

---

[41] https://www.investopedia.com/terms/q/quantitative-easing.asp
[42] https://www.forbes.com/sites/jackbrewster/2020/06/06/there-definitely-will-be-another-stimulus-package-trump-economic-adviser-says/#94e875c3d6da
[43] https://www.unlock-bc.com/news/2020-05-22/china-releases-digital-currency-e-yuan

More immediately worrisome is the coming 2020 US federal election; I pray that a victor is declared without bloodshed. Given the reasons I have mentioned it is highly likely that we will experience another downturn and this one is likely to be protracted.

As I write it occurred to me that a downturn could be truncated or even avoided entirely by cutting military spending in the US. I was thrilled to find out that I was not the only one who had thought of this, as Senator Sanders suggested exactly that, with the also predictable result.[44]

Outside stocks

Every once in a while a person will ask, "What commodities are you buying?"Over the last few years I have always answered, "I like gold and silver right now." And depending on the timing I may include the grains or softs.

If no one has done so yet, let me welcome you to start of our new reality.

There can be no doubt we are in a time of significant change we will see the death of the fossil fuel industry and hopefully the rise of more inclusive humanity.

I hope that you feel have given you some valuable information that will help you.

Whatever awaits us you should be able to apply many of these ideas.

After reading this you might think that I am very pessimistic about our future. I am actually more hopeful than I have been in years that humanity may find a better way. Treating all people as human and fully realizing the power of working together the future could indeed be RADIENT but we shall have to insist!

More on this in my coming trilogy. Book 1 is due out late 2020 and deals with our relationship with currency and where it could go.

---

[44] https://oklahoman.com/article/5667428/senate-defeats-sanders-attempt-to-cut-defense-spending

ESU20 - S&P 500 E-Mini - Daily OHLC Chart

Op:3,111.75, Hi:3,125.25, Lo:3,060.00, Cl:3,108.25

Vol: 1,943,116

ES - S&P 500 E-Mini - Monthly OHLC Chart

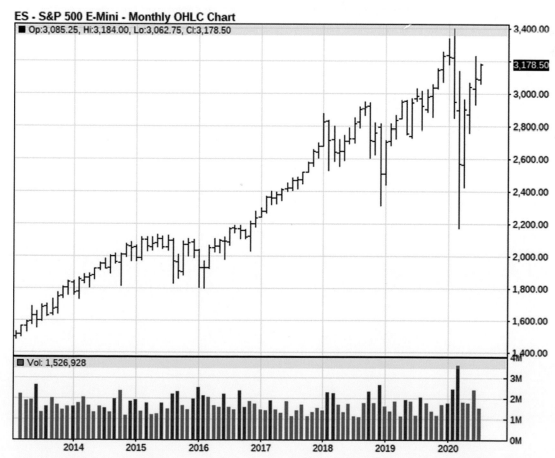

Op:3,085.25, Hi:3,184.00, Lo:3,062.75, Cl:3,178.50

Vol: 1,526,928

<u>Investment plan</u>   Date _____

Account name   _____

Funding account   lump sum/monthly contribution

How much am I ok loosing?   _____

Risk profile?   Low/medium/high

Time Frame   short/medium/long

Investment vehicles?   stocks/mutual funds/bonds/etf/options/futures

Preferred industries if any   _____

Sub-industries?   _____

Preferred vehicles if any   _____

Notes

Goal   _____

APPENDIX A

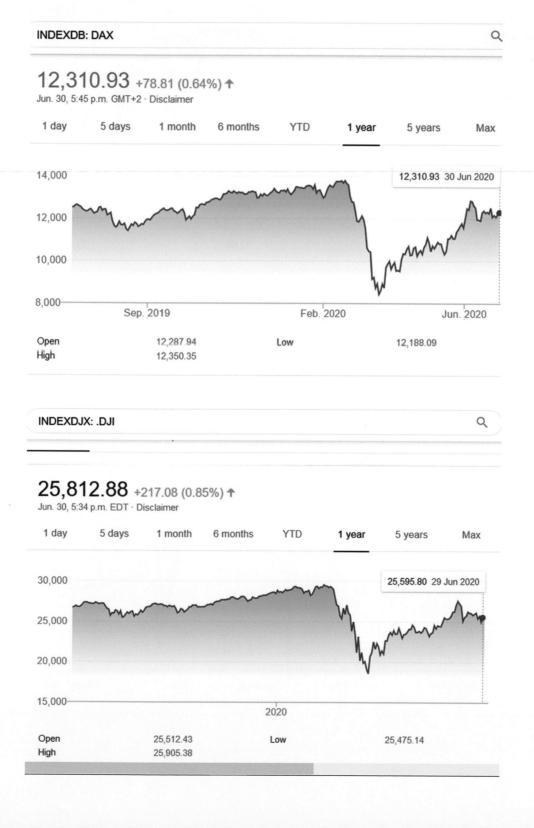

INDEXDB: DAX

12,310.93 +78.81 (0.64%) ↑
Jun. 30, 5:45 p.m. GMT+2 · Disclaimer

| 1 day | 5 days | 1 month | 6 months | YTD | **1 year** | 5 years | Max |

12,310.93 30 Jun 2020

14,000
12,000
10,000
8,000

Sep. 2019   Feb. 2020   Jun. 2020

| Open | 12,287.94 | Low | 12,188.09 |
| High | 12,350.35 | | |

INDEXDJX: .DJI

25,812.88 +217.08 (0.85%) ↑
Jun. 30, 5:34 p.m. EDT · Disclaimer

| 1 day | 5 days | 1 month | 6 months | YTD | **1 year** | 5 years | Max |

25,595.80 29 Jun 2020

30,000
25,000
20,000
15,000

2020

| Open | 25,512.43 | Low | 25,475.14 |
| High | 25,905.38 | | |

INDEXFTSE: UKX 🔍

| 1 day | 5 days | 1 month | 6 months | YTD | **1 year** | 5 years | Max |

Open	6,225.77	Low	6,146.98
High	6,237.51		

🔍 **.N225**   + Comparison   Indicator   Event   🕐 1 Year   ⚏ Daily

▼ ◼ **.N225**   Close 4.83%   7/1/2020

✕ ◼ **.BSESN**

B6 - British Pound - Monthly OHLC Chart

Op:1.2401, Hi:1.2531, Lo:1.2362, Cl:1.2462

Vol: 84,208

Printed in the United States
By Bookmasters